Visit

www.YoungerMeAcademy.com

to request an author visit for your organization, download free coloring pages, watch free video e-books, and more.

If you enjoy this book, please

Leave A Review →

to support our independent family project.

Created by Ben Okon

Illustrated by Jeevankar Bansiwal

For Loula and Owen, two very generous little otters

Special thanks to my professor, Adam Grant, for inspiring this book with his research

Text, art, cover, and logo copyright © 2023 Benjamin Okon, all rights reserved.
Younger Me Academy™ and its logo are trademarks owned by Benjamin Okon, all rights reserved.

Published by Younger Media, LLC
www.youngermeacademy.com

ISBN: 978-1-961428-03-4 (hardcover)

Library of Congress Control Number: 2023910803

All rights reserved. No part of this publication can be reproduced, distributed, or transmitted in any form or by any means without the prior written permission of the copyright holder. This book is intended for interest and entertainment, and does not constitute financial, business, or parenting advice.

Hardcover edition manufactured in China.

The sun began rising in Monterey Bay,
as the water was glistening blue.
The people were strolling alongside the shore
and the animals headed there too.

Seagulls were circling above people's heads
and grabbing some food scraps to eat.
The bees pollinated the flowering beds
while the ducks splashed around with webbed feet.

But the otters were truly the stars of the show.
They flipped and they danced in the bay!
Their smiles were so cute as they swam in pursuit
of a wonderful action-packed day.

An otter named Lou was traveling through.
She was far from her home in these waters.
Now, at her trip's end, she was looking for friends.
She found Owen, a really nice otter.

"Hello to you, Lou! It's nice to meet you!" said Owen to Lou with a smile.

"It's nice to meet **you**! And oh what a view! I think that I'll stay here a while!"

"But, Owen, I'm hungry," said Lou to her friend. "Can you help me get something to eat? I was watching the seagulls. They've figured it out! They get **human** food! Oh, what a treat!"

"Look closer," said Owen, "they're **not** doing great.
The humans just chase them away!
It **seems** like the gulls eat great food till they're full,
but their greed only works for a day.

After a while folks get wise to their game!
They start hiding the best of the stash.
The seagulls get chased from the beach so ashamed,
and they spend all their days eating trash!"

Lou replied, "Wow, I can see that flaw now!
Their snack-stealing can't be the way.
But what about ducks? **Those** guys have luck!
Humans toss them free food in the bay!"

"Ducks don't like dancing! They twirl for a bit, then they eat some stale crumbs and they run. The humans all know ducks just give what they owe, so the food that ducks get isn't fun."

Said Lou, "Generosity can't be the key,
which we know when we look at the bees.
Their days are spent crafting sweet honey for humans,
but they're treated just like a disease!

Humans take beautiful flowers from bees,
but they're awfully scared of those stingers.
The bees try to gift all the fruits of their powers
yet when bees buzz too close, folks don't linger."

"Oh goodness!" said Lou. "Tell me, what do we do?
We're unable to steal, trade, or give.
It all seems so hopeless, and makes me feel blue!
So what is the best way to live?"

"Well," said Owen, "just look at us otters. We're generous, just like the bees. We love to perform for the humans all day, and they give any treats that we please!"

"What's the difference?" asked Lou. "Why's it working for otters, when bees never get what they're due?"

Owen said, "Otters have fun without payment in mind. We can easily dance somewhere new!

Generosity's key to a life of success.
I love giving, and think we all should!
But it can't all be give, 'cause you still have to live!
So give in the ways that feel good."

"Believe it or not, the truth of the plot
is that givers do best in this world.
But givers who don't keep an eye out for takers
may find that their lives can unfurl . . .

Seagulls are greedy 'Takers' *Ducks are tit-for-tat 'Matchers'*

". . . so if you notice you're giving too much,
and others just take with no end,
you'll end up exhausted and get nothing back.
Protect yourself: find a new friend!"

Bees are 'Selfless Givers' *Otters are careful 'Sustained Givers'*

"I get it!" said Lou. "Now I know what to do!"
She swam in the bay and she danced.
The humans threw treats and leapt out of their seats,
and everyone's life was enhanced!

"OLDER ME" ACADEMY
(more about the Science of Generosity for adults and advanced readers)

You've probably heard that it's best to be generous. But how true is it? In his book *Give and Take*, organizational psychologist Adam Grant examined the relative success of three types of people, identified by their attitudes and actions towards others:

- **Givers** (otters and bees) are generous without expecting much in return. The benefits to others outweigh the personal cost.

- **Matchers** (ducks) are willing to give, but expect a return favor to make the personal cost equal to the benefit they receive.

- **Takers** (seagulls) see the world as a competitive place. They want more from others than they are willing to give. The benefits to them are larger than the personal cost.

Give and Take found that Givers achieved the most long-term success in school, careers, sports, etc. Further, their success was contagious—it was more likely that others around them would become Givers. But while many Givers succeeded, others were like bees—they got taken advantage of over the long run and ended up struggling.

So, what's the difference between being a "Sustained Giver" like the otters and a "Selfless Giver" like the bees? Otters are generous in ways that they intrinsically enjoy (dancing), and where they can see, feel, and be energized by the impact of their generosity, so their acts of giving are self-sustaining. If they *do* start to tire, they take a break or find new ways to give that are more revitalizing. They also flexibly adopt a "Matcher" style when confronted with Takers: if they sense they are being taken advantage of, they move their generosity elsewhere. On the other hand:

- **Bees are Selfless Givers.** They give even if they don't enjoy that task, the benefit is unclear, or they are being taken advantage of. Ultimately, even in real life, the bees' approach often leads to burnout.

- **Seagulls are greedy Takers.** They do well in short-term scenarios or brief competitive interactions, but they suck up the energy that others have for giving. In the long term they get chased away.

- **Ducks are Matchers.** They only 'give what they owe.' They are great at protecting themselves from Takers, but they don't create the Giver-like goodwill that drives sustained success.

Even on the playground, the implications of these insights are clear. A child who shares their toys and sees the happiness they bring to others will keep sharing, spreading that generous spirit to others, and will likely end up with a lot of great friends. A child whose toys are not returned will either learn to lend their toys to people who appreciate them, or they will keep losing their toys until they lose the will to keep sharing.

Give and Take concludes that it is, in fact, best to be generous, as long as we steer clear of Takers and are generous in ways that are meaningful to us, impactful for others, and ultimately make us feel good.

Fun fact: Sea otters need food constantly to keep up their energy. They eat about 25% of their weight per day, which is like an adult human eating 75 sandwiches!

The Story Behind Younger Me Academy

Great children's books create special moments that can be shared across generations.

I realized this when my grandmother Gigi, a retired writing teacher, became isolated during COVID-19 with no way to meet my new baby Judah. Instead, we connected over video, where we enjoyed reading Judah's books together.

These moments we shared—the three of us, across nearly 100 years of age—were special, but usually not because of the books. Most books were written for *Judah* without reaching out to pull *me* into his moment as well. They taught him the ABC's, showed him pictures of new things, and told him stories about sharing and friendship.

But I wanted a book that I *could* learn from, too. In particular, I wanted to learn things that I wished I had learned when I was younger, so that Judah and I could grow together. I began writing my own books, and the *Younger Me Academy* was born. Each book is designed to:

- **Help anybody of any age learn and grow** with simplified life-long lessons from science, psychology, business, and beyond.

- **Pull everyone in** (including older readers and younger listeners) through vividly illustrated, character-driven stories written with rhythm and rhyme.

- **Create a deep, special moment** between easily-distracted kids and parents with stories that are long enough to savor but short enough to finish in one fun read.

Younger Me Academy is dedicated to Gigi. Through her writing, teaching, and stories, she inspired me to be a better father, husband, friend, professional, and human. My dream is that this series can continue her legacy by helping other growth-oriented families and their "Younger Me's" to do the same.

Thanks for reading. Please support this independent family project by leaving a book review wherever you found *Younger Me Academy*. I love to learn from you too, so I read every single one.

Ben Okon is a father who never outgrew his childhood habit of asking "why?" and "how?" Now that he has to be the one giving the answers, he loves challenging himself to think through the things he wishes he had known earlier in life from the perspective of a child.

In his spare time, Ben is a business leader who has developed people, product, and corporate strategies with companies like Google, Bain & Co., and Starwood Hotels. He holds an MBA from the Wharton School of Business at the University of Pennsylvania and a BS from the School of Hotel Administration at Cornell University.